THE ESPRESSO SHOT

Joseph Barr

Balboa Press books may be ordered through booksellers or by contacting:

Balboa Press
A Division of Hay House
1663 Liberty Drive
Bloomington, IN 47403
www.balboapress.com
1 (877) 407-4847

ISBN: 978-1-5043-4286-5 (sc)
ISBN: 978-1-5043-4287-2 (e)

Library of Congress Control Number: 2015917668

Print information available on the last page.

Balboa Press rev. date: 10/26/2015

BALBOA
PRESS

A DIVISION OF HAY HOUSE

Prologue

My reason for creating the <u>Espresso Shot</u> is simple, I want to live. These poems were what saved my life, and I wish to share them with you. It is as simple as that. There is nothing here that is *unique* per se. In other words, what is being expressed here are themes that are present within everyone's lives. We live to learn, and we learn so that we may live more fully. This book contains poems of distilled experiences. I didn't so much plan these poems as much as I let them pour out from me. I let them happen on their own. I was the channel. The title of this book comes from my writing style, and the overall goal. I want you to feel charged, and to hopefully experience realization.

I want these poems to be liberation for those who don't yet know their own voices, and a source of supplemental material for those already tapping into their intuition. There is freedom to be had in words, but it should be remembered that the motivations behind the words are far more powerful and important. Words act as symbols, and they transmit an image for our awareness to create knowledge. Our minds, and emotions, are often times misinterpreted to the point of self-mutilation. It is this very misinterpretation that keeps us imprisoned, and erodes the life out of us. I hope these poems help rearrange your internal reality to makes things a little more understandable.

How would I read this booklet? I would go to the table of contents, look at the list of poems, and feel which one resonates. Then I would read the one that resonates. Though in reality one could read the entirety of this book within a single sitting. Take the poems that resonate, and do not "read into them." This is a book to keep on your shelf, or where easily accessible. Read it on days where the air within gets stale. Read it when you need to reconnect with yourself. I have reread these poems and received understanding that I did not see the first few times reading them. As such, I would recommended reading <u>The Espresso Shot</u> multiple times.

So I say now, allow yourself to be open and to feel. Let go of responding to fear with fear, and stop responding to anger with anger. Allow these poems to guide you to the center of yourself with a mind that is willing to heal. Oftentimes realizations come from listening to the story of another, and the self-reflection that occurs automatically.

Enjoy,
Joseph

Table of Contents

Prologue iii

The Child Within.. 1

Forgiveness 4

Peace 5

Momentary Pause 6

Moving On; Moving On..7

My Dream 8

Pride; Pride 9

Singular Experience...10

Strength 11

Nectar..12

The Idea of Failure 14

Outcomes 15

Who am I? 16

Searching for Hope 17

Blame...18

Closure...19

The Reaction; The Response 20

The Maze 21

The Teacher 22

Surprise 23

Farwell For Now 25

The First Kiss 26

The Weight of Purpose 27

Cooperation 28

For All the Love..29

I Am 30

Silent Discovery 31

Eternal 32

Step Out of the Box, and Be Free 33

Epilogue/My Story 36

"What you seek is seeking you"
-Rumi

The Child Within

One day I was walking, step by step, contemplating where I came from. Wondering why I still feel partitioned, a piece of me stuck somewhere in my trail of time. I have walked in many realms, among deserts, forests, along oceans, and mountains. I have seen structures built that have stood the erosion of time, edifices standing for the beliefs of eternity. Still there is an anchor from the past dragging along the sea floor of my existence.

Somewhere among the in-betweens of my journeys, I came upon a child sitting in contemplation while tears slowly trickled to the sand he sat upon. I ask him, "Why are you sitting here all alone?" The boy responded, "I carry a stone in my heart, and with it I cannot see beyond my feet."

This boy I soon realized was myself, and he was asking for my help. Craving the understandings that was not given to him, looking for the hand to hold. Looking for the guidance to create new roots. I understood at that moment, I have an opportunity to give the boy the love he needed, the love that I needed.

I said to the boy, "This stone is not your own, and there is no stone on this Earth that is yours to bear. Let the feelings of sorrow pass through you unhindered and unchanged for they are not yours to keep. Let your light shine through your heart and let it radiate and bathe the gardens you walk in. You are a perfect expression of the intelligence that created this planet. I will lead you to beautiful places that will heal your heart. Take my hand."

The boy stood up and grasped my hand. A bond of unity that was lost somewhere in time, was now rekindled. The boy's stone fell, and my anchor became dislodged.

"Where would you like to go?"

"Lead me to the mountains, where I can see the stars. I have not seen them, and would like to bathe in their light."

As we walked, I pondered the boy's story. Where did he come from, and why of all times do I see him now? As he began to tell his story, I realized I feel him. His sadness is my wince, his joy was my smile. It was as if we lived inseparable, but within two realities, at different stages, but within a universe outside the realm of time. Our journeys are linked, and our ability to communicate with one another was a blessing. Though I realized the timing of the experience was not of my, or the boy's choosing.

"I don't know how to ask for help," the boy began. "Sometimes I ask, "What did I do wrong?" The boy came from a village that shunned him for his beauty. The elders, too caught up in their own woes, tried to love the boy, but always failed in the delivery. The boy eventually became blind of his own beauty, of his own star within, and soon began to treat it with contempt. He did not realize yet the intensity in which he burned.

Forgiveness

Relinquishing the thought of hurt,
giving up on justified denial of the self.
Gathering the patience to sit within,
I can see now the truth.

Communication was hijacked,
by trains from yesteryear,
communication undermined,
by cyclical stories unhealed.

Freedom seemed a lost hope for you,
and only noise seemed to prevail.
You looked to your childhood,
you resented the one who failed you.

I can support you, but I cannot force.
I can grieve with you, but I cannot expect.
Through these cindering ashes of old,
we heal and create something new.

Peace

A cloud's first drop of water,
landing on a sundried brow.
Trailblazing through the salt,
another drop intimately follows.

A ray pears through a cloud,
shimmering on the ocean's face.
A warmth bathing the skin,
in a permeating renewal.

I breathe what unites;
I drink what sustains;
I'm nourished by intelligence;
I rejoice in the company of fellow inhabitants;
I evolve through the grace of compassion.

Momentary Pause

With the essence of wonder,
I sit on my porch and continue to ponder.
Plundering human imagination,
unlocking what it means to inspire.

Higher consciousness forever teasing,
I release the urge the chase.
Looking down only to realize,
a yellow sunflower in its grace.

Understanding my bane for ascension,
sprinting leads only to tribulation.
I kneel with this flower now,
sharing its company in the sun.

An unknown warmth surges,
unlocking a momentary satisfaction.
The creation of a new stencil,
now gives me a place to use my pencil.

Moving On

Lord, sacrifice this wounded scar,
allow it to mutate with eternal essence.
Feed it light, feed it love,
allow this identity to be sated.

Give it what it needs, give it your love,
Lord set me free, heal my child within.
Reverse its polarity, remove the comfort with conflict.
Push it over the edge, push its boundary.

Lord, give me strength to traverse the inertia,
take the sledgehammer of life to the atrocious glass prison.
Shatter the fear, shatter me,
Transform this dysfunction to collaboration.

Give me the grace to see what was shielded,
show me there's something better.
I will not budge from moving on, moving forward,
until you lead my feet in a new direction.

Moving On

I will always remember the love,
I will remember your essence.
I will remember the passionate bliss of your touch,
I move on out of love, I move towards foreign comfort.

You gave me heart, soul, and strength.
You showed the hurt child within,
you showed me my love of life.
I embrace the creation of what now is and cherish.

You showed me love is all there is.
I embraced my rejection of self.
You caressed my tears, and
allowed me room to breathe.

You showed me how to create freedom from my breath,
I showed you how to create fire from placid water.
Now this festive dance must be take its bow,
maybe in another life I will meet you again.

My Dream

From what I thought was needed,
seems to slide down the shoulders,
like water down the spine.
From this basis I push to explore.

I cannot describe a wordless place,
but I can experience it with you.
From the given light in my hand,
I make real the dreams of cravings.

Discern the acceptable from the possible,
and transcend the boundaries together.
Freedom lies within grasp to those who
are open to the universe within.

Creation is the right of free will,
choosing to express that which yearns.
Loving the beyond the effrontery of I,
the dancer is free to play.

A translucent crescendo of loving madness,
boundlessness conceivable only in myth,
I redirect to continue the flow of systemic
implosions of an explosive imagination.

Transforming challenges into potential,
I will hold fast to that which is dear.
This vehicle within an endless adventure,
curtails the night of separation.

Pride

The searing pain of a confession.
What would have been said,
if my perspective was deemed winner?
But my sight was myopic, and broken.

The thought I would lose myself if you were right,
came true when you walked and took meaning with you.
The look in your eyes, and the grimace on your face,
is no prize I ever wish to have again.

Can I ever repair this? Time will only tell.
Regret reminds me of love I could hold,
but now it runs through my hands like water.
Now I must accept what is unchangeable.

Pride

The art of seeing what is mine, and
what is your own imaginary indulgence.
What I used to carry, and shun my eyes to,
has given me the ability to look in your eyes.

Messages I accepted as truth, were
but the lies you hoped for me to believe.
But the dam can only be held back for so long,
and then vision is granted when the seal breaks.

When I learn to see, and accept you for who you are,
I will keep my head up despite the pain in my heart.
Because in the end I'll know I gave it a shot.
That willingness to love, picks me up every time.

Singular Experience

The tearing of old muscle is but
the decay of the inheritance.
Riches come with reinvestment,
allowing me to honor you.

Here with you, I am present.
A sunrise within the mind,
allowing the inky night to be
withdrawn from the eyes.

In this singular experience,
we are the transparent.
You and I are one, and
we look to create ourselves.

As we move in this dance,
we rearrange the stones
with each step we take, and
invite the peace from within.

What you are, is the essence
from which I drink within.
Unity is not our elimination,
but the realization of truth.

Strength

To build I must first break down,
but never taking away from the whole.
The pain from deep was inherited,
freedom comes from transformation.

Even though I may squirm, and run,
I never truly break the perceived chain.
I may push, prod, attack and defend,
but inside my fear has been observed.

The grace of life doesn't allow,
for fear to be permanent.
I am in a place of healing, and
I have been granted a choice.

Judgment may create the bars,
that holds my heart in darkness.
But I chose to cry, and forgive,
I choose to be strong and free.

There are gifts of trauma, and
I no longer shatter from fear.
Rather I am free to create,
within my passive silence.

Nectar

What unfolds is what is meant to be.
The gentlest thing that can be done,
is the choice to walk away from nothing.
Force is the choice of a coward.

Acceptance can mean that I must wait,
and hope another day brings it forward.
As time slips, the erosion of the muscles worsens,
and confusion of what is, shrouds.

In the face of the unknown,
a drought leaves a man begging for water.
Can trust be felt when in the midst of anger?
Oh that dreadful confusion tortures thoughts.

Though when that nectar hits the tongue,
and when the water washes away the salt.
The gifts of the pain begin to shine through,
and one is left saying two words, thank you.

The Idea of Failure

Who am I? The boy once said to himself.
Where do I originate, and what am I to find?
The grey husk that shrouds the mind, always in the future, is
the armor that veils the inner strength, and the self.

Like the genesis of the universe, I am.
However, a lifetime of pain looks to keep
the door of the cell locked, and my soul with it.
What is a boy to do in a veil of tears that are not his own?

Like a lost wondering child of a forgotten home,
I tried to find my way back so many times.
Each home I thought was the final destination,
only to realize it was an imposter clad in illusion.

I felt like a failure at each realization, falling for the minds tricks.
Then once I reached the illusory pinnacle, sure to be home,
I found myself falling again, tumbling down the rabbit hole.
Though once I reached the bottom, something new came.

From a deep well, I naturally began to align with the present.
I made choices to lose the idea of the destination, and future.
I moved into my home, in the now, and lost the grey husk of fear.
This armor, this grey husk, this pain, is the separation of self from itself.

When I found my unity, when I found myself, I found you.
I found myself in you, and an awareness of what is real.
I am that which you seek, and you are that which I seek.
Now in the present, I am no longer imprisoned in the future.

Outcomes

How do I know what is real?
The shades of doubt clog
the cracks that let the light in.
Without light I am blind.

Watching the stepping stones
of my past, leading me to you.
What I thought were failures
was merely the shedding of skin.

The trap of perfection, born from
the fear of pain, a mental prison.
Sight returns to show a masquerade,
what was upside down is made right.

Expectation has no hold here,
allowing potential to unfold.
I bow to the gift of the unknown,
for in it my freedom resides.

The synchronicity of our DNA
comprised of love and pain.
From that which is searching,
I find a sense of myself.

Letting go of fear, I fall.
Falling into the light,
that was always guiding.
Placing me here with you.

Who am I?

I am the reflection that
searches for what really works.
What you call a monster,
I call a child needing answers.

My life was thrown to the side
to provide you with temporary comfort.
Rejection is built upon never
listening to ones closest to you.

I internalized a sense of worthlessness,
so that you would feel comfortable.
I called myself stupid so that you
would talk to me, and you did.

You reinforced an illusion,
rather than saying you are normal.
You would've rather had temporary
relief for yourself because you are blind.

You never provided me with understanding,
instead you lived in self-righteousness.
Foolish I fed into that saint-like devil,
never realizing the internal destruction.

What you are is nothing more than a
child looking for an answer that isn't there.
You served punishment instead of celebration.
This shame will not proceed from here.

Searching for Hope

From the silent place inside,
I observe the pain of change.
The waves of confusion.
Where am I to stand?

The love I seek is the scimitar,
that slices through the scars.
Allowing them to form a new,
I see not beyond the implosions.

Your touch shorts the circuitry,
forcing new channels to be formed.
The pain of friction is only,
the birthing pains into a new reality.

The voice that says I should, or not,
is the voice that ensnares truth.
I know not where the road goes,
for I cannot see beyond my feet.

The fear of letting go, of worth,
says I must force my life into a frame.
Am I only worth the people given?
Where is the road to my heart?

Is it through you? Through waiting?
How the pain sings through the bones,
I know not where to rest, so I walk.
The spark of existence fears what it shouldn't.

Anger of not knowing, attack.
What am I to do? Where are you?
The one that has the touch of life,
where are you?

Blame

What is a child to do when
the ones he looks to pushes him away?
Rather you took my choices and made them
into your pious power trip.

When I wanted more, you stabbed me.
How dare I ask for my birthright?
My life was a paradox of needing
your approval, while not wanting to be you.

I can never be whole in an environment,
that is built upon a façade embedded in shame.
Everything must be avoided, and stuffed down.
Confusion reigned supreme, and I cried.

For years I called myself names, and believed
in interpretations that only served to make
you feel safe in your own skin. Like an
"I told you so" from hell.

It was all in name of blaming everything
on the father of your children. Believing
as if my behavior was a reflection of him.
Never realizing that it was your own shadow.

Closure

We all learn, we all love, and we all fall.
Though the need to regret is delusional.
What needs to be realized is already heard,
and the idea of shame is an enigma.

Past shame, past pain, past choices,
is the humor that instills humility.
Appreciation is born from the ashes,
and the spirits align with harmony.

Chapters open, and chapters close.
Each of them carry phases to see.
Who am I to judge myself? What I
need is right in front of me.

To honor the present, I must honor
the steps that came before this chapter.
Love is the openness to accept anew,
and the ability to heal the scars.

Forgiveness is a two-step game,
and it is not for the weak of heart.
The healing of what was inherited,
and the release from upon myself.

The return of innocence, comes
when love enters to be heard.
And the ultimate realization that
it was truly never taken away.

The Reaction

You never knew who you were,
and it showed in the mirror.
A reaction towards me was a replay
of the sword driven into you.

Your inner child asked your
Son for approval he couldn't give.
A confusion festered in the mind,
and the boy was left searching for love.

How do I live without your permission?
Your shame controls my life, your blind.
I was crushed, left in a repressed reality,
Shaming myself for asking for more.

Anger was left suppressed, and my own
talents were left in the closet.
An identity was superimposed, my life
became subject to external approval.

I oscillated between extremes, always
coming back for your approval, never
did I find a satisfaction with myself.
Now I'm here in a life I built on my own.

The Response

You came to me asking for something
that I simply could not give to you.
I tried to give you what I could,
but I knew it wasn't enough.

I hurt you, yelled at you, broke you.
I ran away, held you at arm's reach,
for the closer you were, the more
pain seared me from the inside.

I was never allowed to love,
because I was never taught how to love.
For you are my son, and though you
are a reflection, I love you.

I never allowed you to understand me,
for I thought I must remain in control.
Fear drove my life, and I made choices
that separated me from myself.

May you let go of the desire for
a connection to occur, for a
life lay waiting at your feet.
You have the opportunity
to create paradise.

Know now you don't have to own
the pain within you any longer.
For approval was never the goal.
May you be free to relinquish.

The Maze

As we enter the maze,
we leave behind a shell.
We begin by exiting the taught,
and enter in a world of unknown.

I turn left, and not right.
I turn right, and not left.
My maze is unique.
My maze is all my own.

My heart thumps with waves,
from the core of essence.
Rippling to give faint direction,
reminding what used to be held.

To find the center, I must listen.
To find boundlessness, I must feel.
For when I listened to another's heart
I lost my way within my maze.

I see now the maze is constructed,
from what was thought, and not my heart.
The maze is a box of boundaries, and tunnels.
My maze is but an illusion of self.

The Teacher

Taking my raw thought,
brimming with emotion.
Removing what is excessive,
and reshaping to create an avenue.

Understanding there is a healing child,
but still seeing straight through the wounds.
Pinpointing the sore bruise,
allowing ownership to create closure.

Teachers always come to the student.
Creating the opportunity,
to traverse what used to be
an insurmountable enigma.

Inner fortitude is your gift,
born out of creative kindness.
Guidance is your talent,
helping to unlock abundance.

Surprise

I never know what I may stumble across,
a fellow traveler, a friend, a teacher, a dream.
A surge that awakens from deep is new in this lifetime,
but is a source of guidance that realigned my soul.

With a smile that enlivens the sunshine, calm follows.
Being in the right place at exactly the right time,
with a spirit that can never be called artificial.
Such is a gift to this planet during a time of need.

May the love that melts the barriers around hearts
be shared, and reciprocated beyond imagining.
I know not where my road leads, but gratitude is restored.
You are the lighthouse that guided me to safe harbor.

Contagious is your smile, and may no person say otherwise.
Courageous actions in the face of uncertainty,
only an intuitive trust was used to recreate a new life.
Rare is this flower in the sun, and may no soul attempt to pluck it.

Farwell For Now

Step by step I walk through life,
feeling the images slid by.
Passing like a curtain over my eyes.
Some images stay within, some leave.

You have come to join me briefly.
Moments of change, renewal, breathe.
Lights danced through our being,
emitted on the dance floor for all to see.

What will I do with your image?
For we seem to be diverging,
a direction that I choose not.
My road is destined in other places.

Perhaps one day we will dance,
among our inner light once again.
I bid a fond farewell, for your
essence will bring light where needed.

The First Kiss

With the grace of composure, you smile as if perfection
only became real with the presence of each other.
The supple joy of your delicate touch singes my senses,
providing peace from an unimaginable depth.

Your legs show the strength of experience and passion,
as if you only knew how to keep walking, not looking back.
Your back conjures class, while blessed with a spine,
that only my touch could unzip, leaving the soul vulnerable.

The flatlands of your stomach gently ripples with breath,
gently signaling the silent depths of a harnessed mind.
May only the finest fabrics be lifted by your breasts,
for I know that such symmetry is seldom seen.

The soft delicacy of your neck, enlivens my pulse,
supported by a jaw line that is firm in its beliefs.
Your cheeks elevate as you peer into my eyes,
smiling with lips pink, and full of craving.

With eyes green as the first spring bloom,
you gaze, silent, thoughtless, and present.
They are doorways to a soul unlocked,
seated within the love and compassion of God.

The Weight of Purpose

Within that single step, the first step,
the mind does not see the past, present or future.
It is a place with no predecessor or repetition.
The essence of what they seek may not be immediate.

Within that single step, boundaries shift, change comes.
No longer has the chooser decided to settle,
and no longer will the chooser avoid their calling.
For in their heart they know a new chapter must be opened.

Within that single step, a journey, a purpose, is accepted.
The chooser no longer resides themselves to an illusion,
and no longer does the chooser cling to the familiar.
For their heart knows life cannot breathe within a jail cell.

Within that single step, perspective changes, a shift occurs.
And no longer does the chooser forgive their own power,
the power within to decide their own fate, their own life.
For in their heart, they no longer wish to forget their love.

Within that single step, a voice is heard.
The voice that whispers through the doubt,
but it is this whisper that speaks to the soul,
for within it carries the weight of purpose.

Cooperation

Release yourself from the stones you are carrying,
for what you carry, I can feel.
May your weary mind sit now with me and forget,
for no soul deserves a cage.

I know not your past, or the road ahead, but I see you.
In this moment I am aware.
I tell you now the pain of fear, and shame is not yours,
and may it rest within the soil below.

This place of wrath and joy is a place of choices
within an interconnected universe.
For what makes you whole, also thrives within my soul,
and no soul deserves a cage.

Isolation removes the potential of self and of others,
I say now, go within and release.
Forgiveness is not for the feeble, but for those willing
to move into the bliss of potential.

Now I ask for you to sit and share what is ensnaring,
and allow me to ease the burden.
May we together bring light and freedom to the voice,
for no soul deserves a cage.

For All the Love

So often I searched for the answers that weren't there.
The questions weren't questions at all, or rather
just simply I had to endure to see a new day, and I prayed.
Now I am here, doubt still a part of my life, but there is a spot.

A chance has arisen, and I have an opportunity to see a new day.
Though doubt, and the unknown shakes the muscles in my legs.
I know not where my road goes, but I hope to have someone
that has the strength in heart to travel it with me.

Dreams have powered me so far, but what happens when that dream is found?
Do I find new ones to create, do I change, where does the road end?
I sit now feeling what could've been, and what lead me to this moment.
So much has been traveled, and I am left feeling, but not seeing the change.

I don't know if the past, present or the future scares me the most.
Though I know I will try, through it all I will try, for love is the journey.
I want the grace to love, and be gentle, at least to the one.
Can I learn compassion? This is the opportunity, and so I jump into the water.

I Am

I hold no ground as my own,
for I am not of this world.
Instant understanding awaits,
those who relinquish identity.

I am a distant traveler,
learning how to set myself free.
Freedom born within,
not swayed by illusion.

The body a humble host.
Inviting an essence from deep,
to sever thought from
its grip on fear.

Moving as water,
I will push for love.
Ascending love's octaves
to experience my purpose.

Silent Discovery

Like being transported to a forgotten time,
I unknowingly reached for your hand.
Like the recreation of a lost temple,
in a world that has forgotten its true identity.

The path of surrender is the path of choice,
and to create is the movement within prayer.
Visualizing the potential, and the sacred, are one.
I travel here to you, in the now, fully awake.

Guidance broke through the unconscious barriers,
carrying a voice saying two words, trust me.
As I reached, as I fell, I cried the tears of all.
The pain of realizing what was meant to be all along.

I sit, and feel, with you here, not in thought,
but rather within the surrender of heart.
A simple movement of surrender, of acceptance,
is the path to realizing the dreams, and purpose of this lifetime.

Eternal

Flowing with the sound of life,
I vibe to the drum of possibility.
Matching the vibration to the freedom within.
Conjuring impossible realities.

Freedom born from the bedrock of gravity,
holding my own while reaching for the sky.
The marriage of everything
in relation to my point of consciousness.

Within a solid world of limits
I meld the pieces to create the solution.
The window of eternity influenced by motivation.
I am my own master capable of anything.

With merely a snap, a new color exists.
Perspectives erased and created within a moment.
Duality is an adjective for what combusts,
creating a birth of paralleled movement that reverberates.

Step Out of the Box, and Be Free

If you would've told me one day I was going to beg, be naked, and be crying at the same time, I probably wouldn't believe you. However, one night not too long ago I found myself doing just that. After becoming fed up with a certain repetitive mental action whose only purpose turns the water murky, I realized something. There is no sin, there is no bad, and there is no lost, only love. When I realized this "Original Sin" was a mental fallacy created by my own actions, love came rushing in. My knees buckled me into a position resembling that of a Muslim praying towards Mecca. Now mind you, for a more complete picture, I had just stepped out of the shower, still dripping with water, and completely vulnerable. God, you sneaky bastard, I love you. I sobbed into a towel that happen to be next to me, and I heaved my lungs until I gasped for air. It felt like I was regurgitating through crying on the white tile floor of my bathroom. Fear was being ripped out of me with the gentle ferocity only God could create.

What was this realization you might ask? The mental structure within the mind yearns for survival. The Ego creates fallacies borne out of insecure conditioned patterns that only today's society could muster, resulting in painful memories and trauma. The Ego continually says life and yourself must be "fixed." Mind you the Ego isn't evil, no not at all. Its "fighting" comes from beliefs constructed from learning that life should be a "certain" way, and it should be experienced in a "certain" way. If reality does not meet these rather primitive standards, the Ego, using your mind, will create responses to create a false reality. The false reality is a blinder that blocks how perfect you are, and leaves you searching for some form of false satisfaction. This apparent stubbornness to change is fueled by unhealed wounds, which in turn is your Ego. The belief that ducking is easier than standing isn't true. Just imagine the idea of never exploring, or trying, or embracing what you were meant to be. But change it must, and change you will. It is your destiny, and it is unavoidable. My advice is to go with it. To put it simply, heal your old memories that still plague you, and watch your life change right in front of your eyes.

The more one realizes the Ego within the mind is only a conditioned structure fueled by trauma, the more empowerment and enlightenment one will ascertain. Follow me so far? It is an individual's duty to help not only themselves but also the rest of humanity. These things go hand in hand. In essence, the more you help yourself the more you help humanity. We are all One, remember? But back to the magic. Love will take your circumstances, however shitty or unpleasant they may be, and it will use them to its advantage so that you praise the day you were born. When you learn to let go of false identity, which is a mental creation, the more love shows you who you are meant to be. Patience is key. Love is lived, Love is a verb. Love is a path before your feet; all you must do is love yourself with each step you take.

You want proof? Look out your window, and watch a bird take a twig from a tree and use it for its home. The tree didn't fight the bird for its property; it gave its essence freely. Watch a flower open; showing its inner vulnerability, which I might add is also its beauty. See how animals, trees, fungi, plants, bacteria, viruses have coevolved to create a web of life that sings. Watch how over millions of years the planet itself shifts its structure to create the magnificent Himalayas. Watch how the animals and microbes coexist with the planet, while the planet itself changes. I tell you these things in order to create gratitude.

When one appreciates life, and impermanence, one realizes who God is. God is your guide. God is the force that helps guide your hands as you conduct your orchestra. God loves you more then you could possibly imagine. God will be there when you fall, encouraging you to get back up (you must choose to get back up, remember that). God surrounds you like a warm blanket on a frigid winter's night. Thank him/her for that, and for his/her essence. What do you think makes this world go round? The insanity of businesses and governments sure as hell doesn't. All you need is love and the courage to live an adventure. Now go to your front door, take a deep breath, and go for a walk.

Thank you,
Joseph

Epilogue/My Story

<u>The Espresso Shot</u> came into creation as a means to heal myself. I believe finding one's own creative outlet is a doorway to unlocking and healing oneself. This small book has been years in the making, and the timing of its finalization (2015) is a reflection of the transition in which I am making in my own life. When I graduated from University, I was lost. Looking back over the years this time period was the deepest part of my 7 year "dark night of the soul".

When I graduated from University I had no job, the job market was abysmal, my parent's violent divorce just ended, I was learning about my codependency/trauma after a break up, I was healing from trauma through EMDR, and I had no money. Through these last 7 years, I was not always aware of this, but I have been on a quest to find myself after a traumatic childhood. I grew up in the archetypal codependent family. The father, an alcoholic/addict, the mother, overcompensated through control and denial. This is also called narcissism. It took years to realize these personalities were a reflection of their own unhealed trauma, but I can only see this after processing my own anger. As such, my life's goal has been the realization of the authentic self.

I began writing poetry as a way to save myself. My Aunt, a person who literally saved my life, suggested I write as a way to process and learn. As she so kindly put it, "you are looking for a savior." I have always been keen on creativity, but it was only during these dark times could I realize its depth. Every time I wrote a poem I transmitted the lesson I needed to learn. I didn't write consciously, all the words were processed from a deep reservoir. The only conscious actions I made were choosing to recognize when I had a poem inside of me waiting to be written.

The central pains of my life revolve around shame, fear, rejection, and abuse. Through these last three years I have continually let go of these emotional issues. No matter how hard one tries you cannot run away from yourself. In other words, no matter how hard you try to be the personality born from these issues, the more one will run into them. It is one's duty to realize the symbolic nature of our careers, relationships, homes, hobbies, habits, and trends. When these issues present themselves we often interpret things in a manner that reinforces these primal issues. We tell ourselves unconsciously that we didn't do well enough, weren't smart enough, or didn't love enough. This state of dissatisfaction is synonymous with the state of constantly needing more. We must learn to interpret these situations, which are a reflection of an emotional issue, in a manner that is open to learning, and letting go. These issues act as magnets to attract situations to be able to see them consciously. In other words, attracting them into your lives is a way of waking up to the deep unconscious emotional issues we all carry.

When we re-approach these issues in self-forgiveness, and compassion, we can heal and move on. This is a journey we all must take.

Within the last year I chose to leave my family. Being connected with my family linked me with my own state of needing "more." In the need of "more," I climbed the administrative ladder, and I realized I yet again attracted an abusive and coercive environment. But I tell you now that there is always a way through. Climbing this ladder gave me resources to a wonderful healer through my work benefits. It was here I was shaken out of denial. We wake up when we are ready to wake up. Up to this point I had written hundreds of poems, and thousands of journal pages, each entry helping me to get to the next step. After months of therapy I met the love of my life. A central theme to my poems, and my ambitions, was to meet the one I truly love. I knew deep down that I would find this person when I found myself. With the departure from my family I was open to finally living my own life, and healing in a new way. Healing in a manner that did not manipulate the framework of my life into the same framework of my family's trauma. It is here I decided to have my poems, and my experience, published.

So it is now I hope you understand that it is ok to be human. It is ok to learn, and it is ok to make mistakes. These mistakes are gateways to a level we did not previously know. So all the fights, the abuse, the violence, the unconscious choices, the times leaving you looking for self-understanding, are all part of the process. So I say now to learn to be your own savior if you already haven't, and know that even though I do not know you, I love you.

This book is dedicated to my Aunt. You gave me the inspiration
to write this book. I love and miss you dearly.

Printed in the United States
By Bookmasters